Fancy Free!
A Kid's Guide to Geiranger, Norway

Photography by John D. Weigand
Poetry by Penelope Dyan

Bellissima Publishing, LLC
Jamul, California
www.bellissimapublishing.com

Copyright © 2018 by Penny D. Weigand & John D. Weigand

All rights reserved. No part of this book may be
reproduced or transmitted in any form or by any means,
electronic or mechanical, including photocopying,
recording, or by any other means, or by any information or
storage retrieval system, without permission from the publisher.

ISBN 978-1-61477-333-7
First Edition

"Half of the fun of a place is getting there, and then you can take a good look around!"

PENELOPE DYAN

Fancy Free!
Bellissima Publishing, LLC

Introduction

Ever Since 2005, the Geirangerfjord area has been listed as a UNESCO World Heritage site! And Geiranger is a place where a kid can have some fun and be amazed all at the same time at the beauty of it all! If this is what you are looking to find, then Geiranger, a small tourist village in Sunnmøre region of Møre og Romsdal county in western Norway, is exactly the place you want to be!

Take a look through the pages of this book, written by the award winning author, attorney and former teacher, Penelope Dyan, and see a bit of what she and our photographer, John D. Weigand saw when they visited this fun place that looks just like it was plucked straight from the pages of a book of fairy tales. (In fact, you might want to look out for the trolls!)

You can also practice your reading skills as you travel though the pages of this kid-sized book (perfect for a kid-sized backpack) because this book is filled with word repetition, word recognition and rhyme. When you are finished reading, you can go to Belissimavideo's YouTube channel and watch the free music video that goes along with this book; and you can see even more of Geiranger, Norway!

Fancy Free!
Bellissima Publishing, LLC

Fancy Free!
A Kid's Guide to Geiranger, Norway

Photography by John D. Weigand
Poetry by Penelope Dyan

Footloose and fancy free,
you look down from the mountain top
to see what you can see!

And near the water, by the shore,
you see and find even more!

There are people camping here.

You see a barn of red.

The beauty of THIS place
fills up YOUR head!

You decide that you are hungry.
You tell your mother
you would like something to eat.
Then your mom buys you
AND your sister
(each) an ice-cream cone sweet!

Then your mother
buys you a friendly moose.

And she buys your sister, Sue,
a cuddly sheep.
You decide that THESE things
are much, much MORE than souvenirs,
because they are memories
you can forever KEEP!

The sights and sounds in Geiranger
fill your imagination,
as you imagine OTHER far off ports
and OTHER far off nations!
You pretend you are a Viking,
pulling up anchor
and sailing far off in a boat on the sea;
and you decide
that IF you COULD only travel
back in time,
a Viking YOU would most assuredly be!

The cars are all in line,
waiting silently to be driven away,
up into the hills
of Geiranger, Norway!
Here the villagers watch
their carbon footprints in the sand;
because they are true
conservationists,
in this far, far off land!
(These cars ARE indeed quite small,
but they DO the job, after ALL!)

You see a boat travel past.
You imagine you are a Viking
And you try to make
the moment last.

Then finally, at the end of the day,
back to the hotel
you, your mom, your dad and your sister
merrily make your way!
And THAT night when YOU go to bed,
thoughts of yourself
as a conquering Viking
begin to fill up your HEAD!
And then you decide
that when you grow up
you will be
the CAPTAIN of a great BIG BOAT,
that travels on the SEA!

"Follow your heart and your imagination, and you can't go wrong!"

PENELOPE DYAN

www.ingramcontent.com/pod-product-compliance
Ingram Content Group UK Ltd.
Pitfield, Milton Keynes, MK11 3LW, UK
UKHW060133240426
12048UKWH00002B/13